CELEBRATION

CW00922279

Harold Pinter was born in L
Antonia Fraser from 1975 ;
1995 he won the David C
awarded for a lifetime's achievement in literature. In 1996
he was given the Laurence Olivier Award for a lifetime's
achievement in theatre. In 2002 he was made a
Companion of Honour for services to literature. In 2005
he was awarded the Nobel Prize for Literature and, in the
same year, the Wilfred Owen Award for Poetry and the
Franz Kafka Award (Prague). In 2006 he was awarded the
Europe Theatre Prize and, in 2007, the highest French
honour, the Légion d'honneur. He died in December 2008.

HAROLD PINTER

Celebration
&
The Room

ff

faber and faber

First published in 2000
by Faber and Faber Limited
Bloomsbury House, 74–77 Great Russell Street,
London WC1B 3DA

Typeset by Country Setting, Kingsdown, Kent CT14 8ES
Printed and bound by CPI Group (UK) Ltd, Croydon, CR0 4YY

Celebration © Harold Pinter, 2000
The Room © Neabar Investments, 1959

The Room was first published by Eyre Methuen in 1960

Harold Pinter is hereby identified as author
of this work in accordance with Section 77
of the Copyright, Designs and Patents Act 1988

A CIP record for this book
is available from the British Library

ISBN 978-0-571-20497-7

Contents

Celebration and **The Room** were first presented as a double bill at the Almeida Theatre, London, on 16 March 2000. The casts were as follows:

Celebration

LAMBERT	Keith Allen
MATT	Andy de la Tour
PRUE	Lindsay Duncan
JULIE	Susan Wooldridge
RUSSELL	Steven Pacey
SUKI	Lia Williams
RICHARD	Thomas Wheatley
SONIA	Indira Varma
WAITER	Danny Dyer
WAITRESS 1	Nina Raine
WAITRESS 2	Katherine Tozer

The Room

ROSE	Lindsay Duncan
BERT	Steven Pacey
MR KIDD	Henry Woolf
MRS SANDS	Lia Williams
MR SANDS	Keith Allen
RILEY	George Harris

Director Harold Pinter
Set Design Eileen Diss
Costume Design Dany Everett
Lighting Mick Hughes
Sound John A. Leonard

CELEBRATION

TABLE ONE

A restaurant. Two curved banquettes.

WAITER

Who's having the duck?

LAMBERT

The duck's for me.

JULIE

No it isn't.

LAMBERT

No it isn't. Who's it for?

JULIE

Me.

LAMBERT

What am I having? I thought I was having the duck?

JULIE

(*to* WAITER) The duck's for me.

MATT

(*to* WAITER) Chicken for my wife, steak for me.

3

WAITER

Chicken for the lady.

PRUE

Thank you so much.

WAITER

And who's having the steak?

MATT

Me.

He picks up a wine bottle and pours.

Here we are. Frascati for the ladies. And Valpolicella for me.

LAMBERT

And for me. I mean what about me? What did I order? I haven't the faintest idea? What did I order?

JULIE

Who cares?

LAMBERT

Who cares? I bloody care.

PRUE

Osso Buco.

LAMBERT

Osso what?

PRUE

Bucco.

MATT

It's an old Italian dish.

LAMBERT

Well I knew Osso was Italian but I know bugger all about Bucco.

MATT

I didn't know arsehole was Italian.

LAMBERT

Yes, but on the other hand what's the Italian for arsehole?

PRUE

Julie, Lambert. Happy anniversary.

MATT

Cheers.

They lift their glasses and drink.

TABLE TWO

RUSSELL

They believe in me.

SUKI

Who do?

RUSSELL

They do. What do you mean, who do? They do.

SUKI

Oh, do they?

RUSSELL

Yes, they believe in me. They reckon me. They're investing in me. In my nous. They believe in me.

SUKI

Listen. I believe you. Honestly. I do. No really, honestly. I'm sure they believe in you. And they're right to believe in you. I mean, listen, I want you to be rich, believe me, I want you to be rich so that you can buy me houses and panties and I'll know that you really love me.

They drink.

RUSSELL

Listen, she was just a secretary. That's all. No more.

SUKI

Like me.

RUSSELL

What do you mean, like you? She was nothing like you.

SUKI

I was a secretary once.

RUSSELL

She was a scrubber. A scrubber. They're all the same, these secretaries, these scrubbers. They're like politicians. They love power. They've got a bit of power, they use it. They go home, they get on the phone, they tell their girlfriends, they have a good laugh. Listen to me. I'm being honest. You won't find many like me. I fell for it. I've admitted it. She just twisted me round her little finger.

SUKI

That's funny. I thought she twisted you round *your* little finger.

Pause.

RUSSELL

You don't know what these girls are like. These secretaries.

SUKI

Oh I think I do.

RUSSELL

You don't.

SUKI

Oh I do.

RUSSELL

What do you mean, you do?

SUKI

I've been behind a few filing cabinets.

RUSSELL

What?

SUKI

In my time. When I was a plump young secretary.
I know what the back of a filing cabinet looks like.

RUSSELL

Oh do you?

SUKI

Oh yes. Listen. I would invest in you myself if I had
any money. Do you know why? Because I believe in
you.

RUSSELL

What's all this about filing cabinets?

SUKI

Oh that was when I was a plump young secretary.
I would never do all those things now. Never. Out
of the question. You see, the trouble was I was so
excitable, their excitement made me so excited, but
I would never do all those things now I'm a grown-up
woman and not a silly young thing, a silly and dizzy
young girl, such a naughty, saucy, flirty, giggly young
thing, sometimes I could hardly walk from one filing
cabinet to another I was so excited, I was so plump
and wobbly it was terrible, men simply couldn't keep
their hands off me, their demands were outrageous,
but coming back to more important things, they're
right to believe in you, why shouldn't they believe in
you?

TABLE ONE

JULIE

I've always told him. Always. But he doesn't listen.
I tell him all the time. But he doesn't listen.

PRUE

You mean he just doesn't listen?

JULIE

I tell him all the time.

PRUE

(*to* LAMBERT) Why don't you listen to your wife? She
stands by you through thick and thin. You've got a
loyal wife there and never forget it.

LAMBERT

I've got a loyal wife where?

PRUE

Here! At this table.

LAMBERT

I've got one under the table, take my tip.

He looks under the table.

Christ. She's really loyal under the table. Always has
been. You wouldn't believe it.

JULIE

Why don't you go and buy a new car and drive it into a brick wall?

LAMBERT

She loves me.

MATT

No, she loves new cars.

LAMBERT

With soft leather seats.

MATT

There was a song once.

LAMBERT

How did it go?

MATT

Aint she neat?
Aint she neat?
As she's walking up the street.
She's got a lovely bubbly pair of tits
And a soft leather seat.

LAMBERT

That's a really beautiful song.

MATT

I've always admired that song. You know what it is?
It's a traditional folk song.

LAMBERT

It's got class.

MATT

It's got tradition and class.

LAMBERT

They don't grow on trees.

MATT

Too bloody right.

LAMBERT

Hey Matt!

MATT

What?

LAMBERT *picks up the bottle of Valpolicella. It is empty.*

LAMBERT

There's something wrong with this bottle.

MATT *turns and calls.*

MATT

Waiter!

TABLE TWO

RUSSELL

All right. Tell me. Do you think I have a nice
character?

SUKI

Yes I think you do. I think you do. I mean I think you
do. Well . . . I mean . . . I think you could have quite
a nice character but the trouble is that when you come
down to it you haven't actually got any character to
begin with – I mean as such, that's the thing.

RUSSELL

As such?

SUKI

Yes, the thing is you haven't really got any character
at all, have you? As such. Au fond. But I wouldn't
worry about it. For example look at me. I don't have
any character either. I'm just a reed. I'm just a reed in
the wind. Aren't I? You know I am. I'm just a reed in
the wind.

RUSSELL

You're a whore.

SUKI

A whore in the wind.

RUSSELL

With the wind blowing up your skirt.

SUKI

That's right. How did you know? How did you know
the sensation? I didn't know that men could possibly
know about that kind of thing. I mean men don't
wear skirts. So I didn't think men could possibly
know what it was like when the wind blows up a
girl's skirt. Because men don't wear skirts.

RUSSELL

You're a prick.

SUKI

Not quite.

RUSSELL

You're a prick.

SUKI

Good gracious. Am I really?

RUSSELL

Yes. That's what you are really.

SUKI

Am I really?

RUSSELL

Yes. That's what you are really.

TABLE ONE

LAMBERT
What's that other song you know? The one you said was a classic.

MATT
Wash me in the water
Where you washed your dirty daughter.

LAMBERT
That's it. (*to* JULIE) Know that one?

JULIE
It's not in my repertoire, darling.

LAMBERT
This is the best restaurant in town. That's what they say.

MATT
That's what they say.

LAMBERT
This is a piss-up dinner. Do you know how much money I made last year?

MATT
I know this is a piss-up dinner.

LAMBERT

It is a piss-up dinner.

PRUE

(*to* JULIE) His mother always hated me. The first time
she saw me she hated me. She never gave me one
present in the whole of her life. Nothing. She wouldn't
give me the drippings off her nose.

JULIE

I know.

PRUE

The drippings off her nose. Honestly.

JULIE

All mothers-in-law are like that. They love their sons.
They love their boys. They don't want their sons to be
fucked by other girls. Isn't that right?

PRUE

Absolutely. All mothers want their sons to be fucked
by themselves.

JULIE

By their mothers.

PRUE

All mothers –

LAMBERT

All mothers want to be fucked by their mothers.

MATT

Or by themselves.

PRUE

No, you've got it the wrong way round.

LAMBERT

How's that?

MATT

All mothers want to be fucked by their sons.

LAMBERT

Now wait a minute –

MATT

My point is –

LAMBERT

No my point is – how old do you have to be?

JULIE

To be what?

LAMBERT

To be fucked by your mother.

MATT

Any age, mate. Any age.

They all drink.

LAMBERT

How did you enjoy your dinner, darling?

JULIE

I wasn't impressed.

LAMBERT

You weren't impressed?

JULIE

No.

LAMBERT

I bring her to the best caff in town – spending a
fortune – and she's not impressed.

MATT

Don't forget this is your anniversary. That's why
we're here.

LAMBERT

What anniversary?

PRUE

It's your wedding anniversary.

LAMBERT

All I know is this is the most expensive fucking
restaurant in town and she's not impressed.

RICHARD *comes to the table.*

RICHARD
Good evening.

MATT
Good evening.

PRUE
Good evening.

JULIE
Good evening.

LAMBERT
Good evening, Richard. How you been?

RICHARD
Very very well. Been to a play?

MATT
No. The ballet.

RICHARD
Oh the ballet? What was it?

LAMBERT
That's a fucking good question.

MATT
It's unanswerable.

RICHARD

Good, was it?

LAMBERT

Unbelievable.

JULIE

What ballet?

MATT

None of them could reach the top notes. Could they?

RICHARD

Good dinner?

MATT

Fantastic.

LAMBERT

Top notch. Gold plated.

PRUE

Delicious.

LAMBERT

My wife wasn't impressed.

RICHARD

Oh really?

JULIE

I liked the waiter.

RICHARD
Which one?

JULIE
The one with the fur-lined jockstrap.

LAMBERT
He takes it off for breakfast.

JULIE
Which is more than you do.

RICHARD
Well how nice to see you all.

PRUE
She wasn't impressed with her food. It's true. She said so. She thought it was dry as dust. She said – what did you say darling? – she's my sister – she said she could cook better than that with one hand stuffed between her legs – she said – no, honestly – she said she could make a better sauce than the one on that plate if she pissed into it. Don't think she was joking – she's my sister, I've known her all my life, all my life, since we were little innocent girls, all our lives, when we were babies, when we used to lie in the nursery and hear mummy beating the shit out of daddy. We saw the blood on the sheets the next day – when nanny was in the pantry – my sister and me – and nanny was in the pantry – and the pantry maid was in the larder and the parlour maid was in the laundry room washing

the blood out of the sheets. That's how my little sister and I were brought up and she could make a better sauce than yours if she pissed into it.

MATT

Well, it's lovely to be here, I'll say that.

LAMBERT

Lovely to be here.

JULIE

Lovely. Lovely.

MATT

Really lovely.

RICHARD

Thank you.

PRUE *stands and goes to* RICHARD.

PRUE

Can I thank you? Can I thank you personally? I'd like to thank you myself, in my own way.

RICHARD

Well thank you.

PRUE

No no, I'd really like to thank you in a very personal way.

JULIE

She'd like to give you her personal thanks.

PRUE

Will you let me kiss you? I'd like to kiss you on the mouth?

JULIE

That's funny. I'd like to kiss him on the mouth too.

She stands and goes to him.

Because I've been maligned, I've been misrepresented. I never said I didn't like your sauce. I love your sauce.

PRUE

We can't both kiss him on the mouth at the same time.

LAMBERT

You could tickle his arse with a feather.

RICHARD

Well I'm so glad. I'm really glad. See you later I hope.

He goes. PRUE *and* JULIE *sit.*

Silence.

MATT

Charming man.

LAMBERT

That's why this is the best and most expensive
restaurant in the whole of Europe – because he *insists*
upon proper standards, he *insists* that standards are
maintained with the utmost rigour, you get me? That
standards are maintained up to the highest standards,
up to the very highest fucking standards –

MATT

He doesn't jib.

LAMBERT

Jib? Of course he doesn't jib – it would be more than
his life was worth. He jibs at nothing!

PRUE

I knew him in the old days.

MATT

What do you mean?

PRUE

When he was a chef.

Lambert's mobile phone rings.

LAMBERT

Who the fuck's this?

He switches it on.

Yes? What?

He listens briefly.

I said no calls! It's my fucking wedding anniversary!

He switches it off.

Cunt.

TABLE TWO

SUKI
I'm so proud of you.

RUSSELL
Yes?

SUKI
And I know these people are good people. These people who believe in you. They're good people. Aren't they?

RUSSELL
Very good people.

SUKI
And when I meet them, when you introduce me to them, they'll treat me with respect, won't they? They won't want to fuck me behind a filing cabinet?

SONIA *comes to the table.*

SONIA
Good evening.

RUSSELL
Good evening.

SUKI

Good evening.

SONIA

Everything all right?

RUSSELL

Wonderful.

SONIA

No complaints?

RUSSELL

Absolutely no complaints whatsoever. Absolutely
numero uno all along the line.

SONIA

What a lovely compliment.

RUSSELL

Heartfelt.

SONIA

Been to the theatre?

SUKI

The opera.

SONIA

Oh really, what was it?

SUKI

Well . . . there was a lot going on. A lot of singing.
A great deal, as a matter of fact. They never stopped.
Did they?

RUSSELL

(*to* SONIA) Listen, let me ask you something.

SONIA

You can ask me absolutely anything you like.

RUSSELL

What was your upbringing?

SONIA

That's funny. Everybody asks me that. Everybody
seems to find that an interesting subject. I don't know
why. Isn't it funny? So many people express curiosity
about my upbringing. I've no idea why. What you
really mean of course is – how did I arrive at the
position I hold now – maitresse d'hotel – isn't that
right? Isn't that your question? Well, I was born in
Bethnal Green. My mother was a chiropodist. I had
no father.

RUSSELL

Fantastic.

SONIA

Are you going to try our bread-and-butter pudding?

RUSSELL

In spades.

SONIA *smiles and goes.*

RUSSELL

Did I ever tell you about my mother's bread-and-butter pudding?

SUKI

You never have. Please tell me.

RUSSELL

You really want me to tell you? You're not being insincere?

SUKI

Darling. Give me your hand. There. I have your hand. I'm holding your hand. Now please tell me. Please tell me about your mother's bread-and-butter pudding. What was it like?

RUSSELL

It was like drowning in an ocean of richness.

SUKI

How beautiful. You're a poet.

RUSSELL

I wanted to be a poet once. But I got no encouragement from my dad. He thought I was an arsehole.

SUKI

He was jealous of you, that's all. He saw you as a
threat. He thought you wanted to steal his wife.

RUSSELL

His wife?

SUKI

Well, you know what they say.

RUSSELL

What?

SUKI

Oh, you know what they say.

The WAITER *comes to the table and pours wine.*

WAITER

Do you mind if I interject?

RUSSELL

Eh?

WAITER

I say, do you mind if I make an interjection?

SUKI

We'd welcome it.

WAITER

It's just that I heard you talking about T. S. Eliot a
little bit earlier this evening.

SUKI

Oh you heard that, did you?

WAITER

I did. And I thought you might be interested to know
that my grandfather knew T. S. Eliot quite well.

SUKI

Really?

WAITER

I'm not claiming that he was a close friend of his.
But he was a damn sight more than a nodding
acquaintance. He knew them all in fact, Ezra Pound,
W. H. Auden, C. Day Lewis, Louis MacNeice,
Stephen Spender, George Barker, Dylan Thomas and
if you go back a few years he was a bit of a drinking
companion of D. H. Lawrence, Joseph Conrad,
Ford Madox Ford, W. B. Yeats, Aldous Huxley,
Virginia Woolf and Thomas Hardy in his dotage.
My grandfather was carving out a niche for himself
in politics at the time. Some saw him as a future
Chancellor of the Exchequer or at least First Lord
of the Admiralty but he decided instead to command
a battalion in the Spanish Civil War but as things
turned out he spent most of his spare time in the
United States where he was a very close pal of Ernest

Hemingway – they used to play gin rummy together
until the cows came home. But he was also boon
compatriots with William Faulkner, Scott Fitzgerald,
Upton Sinclair, John Dos Passos – you know – that
whole vivid Chicago gang – not to mention John
Steinbeck, Erskine Caldwell, Carson McCullers and
other members of the old Deep South conglomerate.
I mean – what I'm trying to say is – that as a man my
grandfather was just about as all round as you can
get. He was never without his pocket bible and he was
a dab hand at pocket billiards. He stood four square
in the centre of the intellectual and literary life of the
tens, twenties and thirties. He was James Joyce's
godmother.

Silence.

RUSSELL
Have you been working here long?

WAITER
Years.

RUSSELL
You going to stay until it changes hands?

WAITER
Are you suggesting that I'm about to get the boot?

SUKI
They wouldn't do that to a nice lad like you.

WAITER

To be brutally honest, I don't think I'd recover if they did a thing like that. This place is like a womb to me. I prefer to stay in my womb. I strongly prefer that to being born.

RUSSELL

I don't blame you. Listen, next time we're talking about T. S. Eliot I'll drop you a card.

WAITER

You would make me a very happy man. Thank you. Thank you. You are incredibly gracious people.

SUKI

How sweet of you.

WAITER

Gracious and graceful.

He goes.

SUKI

What a nice young man.

TABLE ONE

LAMBERT

You won't believe this. You're not going to believe this – and I'm only saying this because I'm among friends – and I know I'm well liked because I trust my family and my friends – because I know they like me fundamentally – you know – deep down they trust me – deep down they respect me – otherwise I wouldn't say this. I wouldn't take you all into my confidence if I thought you all hated my guts – I couldn't be open and honest with you if I thought you thought I was a pile of shit. If I thought you would like to see me hung, drawn and fucking quartered – I could never be frank and honest with you if that was the truth – never . . .

Silence.

But as I was about to say, you won't believe this, I fell in love once and this girl I fell in love with loved me back. I know she did.

Pause.

JULIE

Wasn't that me, darling?

LAMBERT

Who?

MATT

Her.

LAMBERT

Her? No, not her. A girl. I used to take her for walks along the river.

JULIE

Lambert fell in love with me on the top of a bus. It was a short journey. Fulham Broadway to Shepherd's Bush, but it was enough. He was trembling all over. I remember. (*to* PRUE) When I got home I came and sat on your bed, didn't I?

LAMBERT

I used to take this girl for walks along the river. I was young, I wasn't much more than a nipper.

MATT

That's funny. I never knew anything about that. And I knew you quite well, didn't I?

LAMBERT

What do you mean you knew me quite well? You knew nothing about me. You know nothing about me. Who the fuck are you anyway?

MATT

I'm your big brother.

LAMBERT

I'm talking about love, mate. You know, real fucking love, walking along the banks of a river holding hands.

MATT

I saw him the day he was born. You know what he looked like? An alcoholic. Pissed as a newt. He could hardly stand.

JULIE

He was trembling like a leaf on top of that bus. I'll never forget it.

PRUE

I was there when you came home. I remember what you said. You came into my room. You sat down on my bed.

MATT

What did she say?

PRUE

I mean we were sisters, weren't we?

MATT

Well, what did she say?

PRUE

I'll never forget what you said. You sat on my bed. Didn't you? Do you remember?

LAMBERT

This girl was in love with me – I'm trying to tell you.

PRUE

Do you remember what you said?

TABLE TWO

Richard comes to the table.

RICHARD

Good evening.

RUSSELL

Good evening.

SUKI

Good evening.

RICHARD

Everything in order?

RUSSELL

First class.

RICHARD

I'm so glad.

SUKI

Can I say something?

RICHARD

But indeed –

SUKI

Everyone is so happy in your restaurant. I mean women *and* men. You make people so happy.

RICHARD

Well, we do like to feel that it's a happy restaurant.

RUSSELL

It is a happy restaurant. For example, look at me. Look at me. I'm basically a totally disordered personality, some people would describe me as a psychopath. (*to* SUKI) Am I right?

SUKI

Yes.

RUSSELL

But when I'm sitting in this restaurant I suddenly find I have no psychopathic tendencies at all. I don't feel like killing everyone in sight, I don't feel like putting a bomb under everyone's arse. I feel something quite different, I have a sense of equilibrium, of harmony, I love my fellow diners. Now this is very unusual for me. Normally I feel – as I've just said – absolutely malice and hatred towards everyone within spitting distance – but here I feel love. How do you explain it?

SUKI

It's the ambience.

RICHARD

Yes, I think ambience is that intangible thing that cannot be defined.

RUSSELL

Quite right.

SUKI

It is intangible. You're absolutely right.

RUSSELL

Absolutely.

RICHARD

That is absolutely right. But it does – I would freely admit – exist. It's something you find you are part of. Without knowing exactly what it is.

RUSSELL

Yes. I had an old schoolmaster once who used to say that ambience surrounds you. He never stopped saying that. He lived in a little house in a nice little village but none of us boys were ever invited to tea.

RICHARD

Yes, it's funny you should say that. I was brought up in a little village myself.

SUKI

No? Were you?

RICHARD

Yes, isn't it odd? In a little village in the country.

RUSSELL

What, right in the country?

RICHARD

Oh, absolutely. And my father once took me to our
village pub. I was only that high. Too young to join
him for his pint of course. But I did look in. Black
beams.

RUSSELL

On the roof?

RICHARD

Well, holding the ceiling up in fact. Old men smoking
pipes, no music of course, cheese rolls, gherkins,
happiness. I think this restaurant – which you so
kindly patronise – was inspired by that pub in my
childhood. I do hope you noticed that you have
complimentary gherkins as soon as you take your
seat.

SUKI

That was you! That was your idea!

RICHARD

I believe the concept of this restaurant rests in that
public house of my childhood.

SUKI

I find that incredibly moving.

TABLE ONE

LAMBERT

I'd like to raise my glass.

MATT

What to?

LAMBERT

To my wife. To our anniversary.

JULIE

Oh darling! You remembered!

LAMBERT

I'd like to raise my glass. I ask you to raise your
glasses to my wife.

JULIE

I'm so touched by this, honestly. I mean I have to
say –

LAMBERT

Raise your fucking glass and shut up!

JULIE

But darling, that's naked aggression. He doesn't
normally go in for naked aggression. He usually
disguises it under honeyed words. What is it sweetie?
He's got a cold in the nose, that's what it is.

LAMBERT

I want us to drink to our anniversary. We've been married for more bloody years than I can remember and it don't seem a day too long.

PRUE

Cheers.

MATT

Cheers.

JULIE

It's funny our children aren't here. When they were young we spent so much time with them, the little things, looking after them.

PRUE

I know.

JULIE

Playing with them.

PRUE

Feeding them.

JULIE

Being their mothers.

PRUE

They always loved me much more than they loved him.

JULIE

Me too. They loved me to distraction. I was their
mother.

PRUE

Yes, I was too. I was my children's mother.

MATT

They have no memory.

LAMBERT

Who?

MATT

Children. They have no memory. They remember
nothing. They don't remember who their father was
or who their mother was. It's all a hole in the wall for
them. They don't remember their own life.

SONIA *comes to the table.*

SONIA

Everything all right?

JULIE

Perfect.

SONIA

Were you at the opera this evening?

JULIE

No.

PRUE

No.

SONIA

Theatre?

PRUE

No.

JULIE

No.

MATT

This is a celebration.

SONIA

Oh my goodness! A birthday?

MATT

Anniversary.

PRUE

My sister and her husband. Anniversary of their
marriage. I was her leading bridesmaid.

MATT

I was his best man.

LAMBERT

I was just about to fuck her at the altar when
somebody stopped me.

SONIA

Really?

MATT

I stopped him. His zip went down and I kicked him
up the arse. It would have been a scandal. The world's
press was on the doorstep.

JULIE

He was always impetuous.

SONIA

We get so many different kinds of people in here,
people from all walks of life.

PRUE

Do you really?

SONIA

Oh yes. People from all walks of life. People from
different countries. I've often said, 'You don't have
to speak English to enjoy good food.' I've often said
that. Or even understand English. It's like sex isn't it?
You don't have to be English to enjoy sex. You don't
have to speak English to enjoy sex. Lots of people
enjoy sex without being English. I've known one or
two Belgian people for example who love sex and
they don't speak a word of English. The same applies
to Hungarians.

LAMBERT

Yes. I met a chap who was born in Venezuela once and he didn't speak a fucking word of English.

MATT

Did he enjoy sex?

LAMBERT

Sex?

SONIA

Yes, it's funny you should say that. I met a man from Morocco once and he was very interested in sex.

JULIE

What happened to him?

SONIA

Now you've upset me. I think I'm going to cry.

PRUE

Oh, poor dear. Did he let you down?

SONIA

He's dead. He died in another woman's arms. He was on the job. Can you see how tragic my life has been?

Pause.

MATT

Well, I can. I don't know about the others.

JULIE

I can too.

PRUE

So can I.

SONIA

Have a happy night.

She goes.

LAMBERT

Lovely woman.

The WAITER *comes to the table and pours wine into their glasses.*

WAITER

Do you mind if I interject?

MATT

What?

WAITER

Do you mind if I make an interjection?

MATT

Help yourself.

WAITER

It's just that a little bit earlier I heard you saying

something about the Hollywood studio system in the
thirties.

PRUE

Oh you heard that?

WAITER

Yes. And I thought you might be interested to know
that my grandfather was very familiar with a lot of
the old Hollywood film stars back in those days. He
used to knock about with Clark Gable and Elisha
Cook Jr and he was one of the very few native-born
Englishmen to have had it off with Hedy Lamarr.

JULIE

No?

LAMBERT

What was she like in the sack?

WAITER

He said she was really tasty.

JULIE

I'll bet she was.

WAITER

Of course there was a very well-established Irish
Mafia in Hollywood in those days. And there was a
very close connection between some of the famous
Irish film stars and some of the famous Irish gangsters

in Chicago. Al Capone and Victor Mature for example.
They were both Irish. Then there was John Dillinger
the celebrated gangster and Gary Cooper the celebrated
film star. They were Jewish.

Silence.

JULIE

It makes you think, doesn't it?

PRUE

It does make you think.

LAMBERT

You see that girl at that table? I know her. I fucked
her when she was eighteen.

JULIE

What, by the banks of the river?

LAMBERT *waves at* SUKI. SUKI *waves back. She
whispers to* RUSSELL, *gets up and goes to Lambert's
table followed by* RUSSELL.

SUKI

Lambert! It's you!

LAMBERT

Suki! You remember me!

SUKI

Do you remember me?

LAMBERT

Do I remember you? *Do* I remember you!

SUKI

This is my husband Russell.

LAMBERT

Hello Russell.

RUSSELL

Hello Lambert.

LAMBERT

This is my wife Julie.

JULIE

Hello Suki.

SUKI

Hello Julie.

RUSSELL

Hello Julie.

JULIE

Hello Russell.

LAMBERT

And this is my brother Matt.

MATT

Hello Suki, hello Russell.

SUKI

Hello Matt.

RUSSELL

Hello Matt.

LAMBERT

And this is his wife Prue. She's Julie's sister.

SUKI

She's not!

PRUE

Yes, we're sisters and they're brothers.

SUKI

They're not!

RUSSELL

Hello Prue.

PRUE

Hello Russell.

SUKI

Hello Prue.

PRUE

Hello Suki.

LAMBERT

Sit down. Squeeze in. Have a drink.

They sit.

What'll you have?

RUSSELL

A drop of that red wine would work wonders.

LAMBERT

Suki?

RUSSELL

She'll have the same.

SUKI

(*to* LAMBERT) Are you still obsessed with gardening?

LAMBERT

Me?

SUKI

(*to* JULIE) When I knew him he was absolutely
obsessed with gardening.

LAMBERT

Yes, well, I would say I'm still moderately obsessed
with gardening.

JULIE

He likes grass.

LAMBERT

It's true. I love grass.

JULIE

Green grass.

SUKI

You used to love flowers, didn't you? Do you still love flowers?

JULIE

He adores flowers. The other day I saw him emptying a piss pot into a bowl of lilies.

RUSSELL

My dad was a gardener.

MATT

Not your grandad?

RUSSELL

No, my dad.

SUKI

That's right, he was. He was always walking about with a lawn mower.

LAMBERT

What, even in the Old Kent Road?

RUSSELL

He was a man of the soil.

MATT

How about your grandad?

RUSSELL

I never had one.

JULIE

Funny that when you knew my husband you thought he was obsessed with gardening. I always thought he was obsessed with girls' bums.

SUKI

Really?

PRUE

Oh yes, he was always a keen wobbler.

MATT

What do you mean? How do you know?

PRUE

Oh don't get excited. It's all in the past.

MATT

What is?

SUKI

I sometimes feel that the past is never past.

RUSSELL

What do you mean?

JULIE

You mean that yesterday is today?

SUKI

That's right. You feel the same, do you?

JULIE

I do.

MATT

Bollocks.

JULIE

I wouldn't like to live again though, would you? Once is more than enough.

LAMBERT

I'd like to live again. In fact I'm going to make it my job to live again. I'm going to come back as a better person, a more civilised person, a gentler person, a nicer person.

JULIE

Impossible.

Pause.

PRUE

I wonder where these two met? I mean Lambert and Suki.

RUSSELL

Behind a filing cabinet.

Silence.

JULIE

What is a filing cabinet?

RUSSELL

It's a thing you get behind.

Pause.

LAMBERT

No, not me mate. You've got the wrong bloke. I agree with my wife. I don't even know what a filing cabinet looks like. I wouldn't know a filing cabinet if I met one coming round the corner.

Pause.

JULIE

So what's your job now then, Suki?

SUKI

Oh, I'm a schoolteacher now. I teach infants.

PRUE

What, little boys and little girls?

SUKI

What about you?

PRUE

Oh, Julie and me – we run charities. We do charities.

RUSSELL

Must be pretty demanding work.

JULIE

Yes, we're at it day and night, aren't we?

PRUE

Well, there are so many worthy causes.

MATT

(*to* RUSSELL) You're a banker? Right?

RUSSELL

That's right.

MATT

(*to* LAMBERT) He's a banker.

LAMBERT

With a big future before him.

MATT

Well that's what he reckons.

LAMBERT

I want to ask you a question. How did you know he
was a banker?

MATT

Well it's the way he holds himself, isn't it?

LAMBERT

Oh, yes.

SUKI

What about you two?

LAMBERT

Us two?

SUKI

Yes.

LAMBERT

Well, we're consultants. Matt and me. Strategy consultants.

MATT

Strategy consultants.

LAMBERT

It means we don't carry guns.

MATT *and* LAMBERT *laugh*.

We don't have to!

MATT

We're peaceful strategy consultants.

LAMBERT

Worldwide. Keeping the peace.

RUSSELL

Wonderful.

LAMBERT

Eh?

RUSSELL

Really impressive. We need a few more of you about.

Pause.

We need more people like you. Taking responsibility.
Taking charge. Keeping the peace. Enforcing the
peace. Enforcing peace. We need more like you.
I think I'll have a word with my bank. I'm moving
any minute to a more substantial bank. I'll have
a word with them. I'll suggest lunch. In the City.
I know the ideal restaurant. All the waitresses have
big tits.

SUKI

Aren't you pushing the tits bit a bit far?

RUSSELL

Me? I thought you did that.

Pause.

LAMBERT

Be careful. You're talking to your wife.

MATT

Have some respect, mate.

LAMBERT

Have respect. That's all we ask.

MATT

It's not much to ask.

LAMBERT

But it's crucial.

Pause.

RUSSELL
So how is the strategic consultancy business these days?

LAMBERT
Very good, old boy. Very good.

MATT
Very good. We're at the receiving end of some of the best tea in China.

RICHARD *and* SONIA *come to the table with a magnum of champagne, the* WAITER *with a tray of glasses. Everyone gasps.*

RICHARD
To celebrate a treasured wedding anniversary.

MATT *looks at the label on the bottle.*

MATT
That's the best of the best.

The bottle opens. RICHARD *pours.*

LAMBERT
And may the best man win!

JULIE
The woman always wins.

PRUE

Always.

SUKI

That's really good news.

PRUE

The woman always wins.

RICHARD *and* SONIA *raise their glasses.*

RICHARD

To the happy couple. God bless. God bless you all.

EVERYONE

Cheers. Cheers . . .

MATT

What a wonderful restaurant this is.

SONIA

Well, we do care. I will say that. We care. That's the point. Don't we?

RICHARD

Yes. We do care. We care about the welfare of our clientele. I will say that.

LAMBERT *stands and goes to them.*

LAMBERT
What you say means so much to me. Let me give you
a cuddle.

He cuddles RICHARD.

And let me give you a cuddle.

He cuddles SONIA.

This is so totally rare, you see. None of this normally
happens. People normally – you know – people
normally are so distant from each other. That's what
I've found. Take a given bloke – this given bloke
doesn't know that another given bloke exists. It goes
down through history, doesn't it?

MATT
It does.

LAMBERT
One bloke doesn't know that another bloke exists.
Generally speaking. I've often noticed.

SONIA
(*to* JULIE *and* PRUE) I'm so touched that you're
sisters. I had a sister. But she married a foreigner and
I haven't seen her since.

PRUE
Some foreigners are all right.

SONIA

Oh I think foreigners are charming. Most people
in this restaurant tonight are foreigners. My sister's
husband had a lot of charm but he also had an
enormous moustache. I had to kiss him at the
wedding. I can't describe how awful it was. I've
got such soft skin, you see.

WAITER

Do you mind if I interject?

RICHARD

I'm sorry?

WAITER

Do you mind if I make an interjection?

RICHARD

What on earth do you mean?

WAITER

Well, it's just that I heard all these people talking
about the Austro-Hungarian Empire a little while
ago and I wondered if they'd ever heard about my
grandfather. He was an incredibly close friend of the
Archduke himself and he once had a cup of tea with
Benito Mussolini. They all played poker together,
Winston Churchill included. The funny thing about
my grandfather was that the palms of his hands
always seemed to be burning. But his eyes were
elsewhere. He had a really strange life. He was in

love, he told me, once, with the woman who turned
out to be my grandmother, but he lost her somewhere.
She disappeared, I think, in a sandstorm. In the desert.
My grandfather was everything men aspired to be in
those days. He was tall, dark and handsome. He was
full of good will. He'd even give a cripple with no legs
crawling on his belly through the slush and mud of a
country lane a helping hand. He'd lift him up, he'd
show him his way, he'd point him in the right direction.
He was like Jesus Christ in that respect. And he was
gregarious. He loved the society of his fellows, W. B.
Yeats, T. S. Eliot, Igor Stravinsky, Picasso, Ezra Pound,
Bertholt Brecht, Don Bradman, the Beverley Sisters,
the Inkspots, Franz Kafka and the Three Stooges. He
knew these people where they were isolated, where
they were alone, where they fought against savage and
pitiless odds, where they suffered vast wounds to their
bodies, their bellies, their legs, their trunks, their eyes,
their throats, their breasts, their balls –

LAMBERT
(*standing*) Well, Richard – what a great dinner!

RICHARD
I'm so glad.

LAMBERT *opens his wallet and unpeels fifty-pound
notes. He gives two to* RICHARD.

LAMBERT
This is for you.

RICHARD
No, no really –

LAMBERT
No no, this is for you. (*to* SONIA) And this is for you.

SONIA
Oh, no please –

LAMBERT *dangles the notes in front of her cleavage.*

LAMBERT
Shall I put them down here?

SONIA *giggles.*

No I'll tell you what – you wearing suspenders?

SONIA *giggles.*

Stick them in your suspenders. (*to* WAITER) Here you are son. Mind how you go.

Puts a note into his pocket.

Great dinner. Great restaurant. Best in the country.

MATT
Best in the world I'd say.

LAMBERT

Exactly. (*to* RICHARD) I'm taking their bill.

RUSSELL

No, no you can't –

LAMBERT

It's my wedding anniversary! Right? (*to* RICHARD)
Send me their bill.

JULIE

And his.

LAMBERT

Send me both bills. Anyway . . .

He embraces SUKI.

It's for old time's sake as well, right?

SUKI

Right.

RICHARD

See you again soon?

MATT

Absolutely.

SONIA

See you again soon.

PRUE

Absolutely.

SONIA

Next celebration?

JULIE

Absolutely.

LAMBERT

Plenty of celebrations to come. Rest assured.

MATT

Plenty to celebrate.

LAMBERT

Dead right.

MATT *slaps his thighs.*

MATT

Like – who's in front? Who's in front?

LAMBERT *joins in the song, slapping his thighs in time with* MATT.

LAMBERT AND MATT

Who's in front?
Who's in front?

HAROLD PINTER

LAMBERT

Get out the bloody way
You silly old cunt!

LAMBERT *and* MATT *laugh.*

SUKI *and* RUSSELL *go to their table to collect
handbag and jacket, etc.*

SUKI

How sweet of him to take the bill, wasn't it?

RUSSELL

He must have been very fond of you.

SUKI

Oh he wasn't all that fond of me really. He just liked
my . . . oh . . . you know . . .

RUSSELL

Your what?

SUKI

Oh . . . my . . . you know . . .

LAMBERT

Fabulous evening.

JULIE

Fabulous.

RICHARD

See you soon then.

SONIA

See you soon.

MATT

I'll be here for breakfast tomorrow morning.

SONIA

Excellent!

PRUE

See you soon.

SONIA

See you soon.

JULIE

Lovely to see you.

SONIA

See you soon I hope.

RUSSELL

See you soon.

SUKI

See you soon.

They drift off.

JULIE (*off*)

So lovely to meet you.

SUKI (*off*)

Lovely to meet you.

Silence.

The WAITER *stands alone.*

WAITER

When I was a boy my grandfather used to take me
to the edge of the cliffs and we'd look out to sea.
He bought me a telescope. I don't think they have
telescopes any more. I used to look through this
telescope and sometimes I'd see a boat. The boat
would grow bigger through the telescopic lens.
Sometimes I'd see people on the boat. A man,
sometimes, and a woman, or sometimes two men.
The sea glistened.

My grandfather introduced me to the mystery of life
and I'm still in the middle of it. I can't find the door
to get out. My grandfather got out of it. He got right
out of it. He left it behind him and he didn't look back.

He got that absolutely right.

And I'd like to make one further interjection.

He stands still.

Slow fade.

THE ROOM

The Room was first presented at The University of
Bristol Department of Drama on 15 May 1957 with
the following cast:

BERT HUDD	Claude Jenkins
ROSE HUDD	Susan Engel
MR KIDD	Henry Woolf
MR SANDS	David Davies
MRS SANDS	Auriol Smith
RILEY	George Odlum

Directed by Henry Woolf

The Room was subsequently presented at The
Hampstead Theatre Club on 21 January 1960 with
the following cast:

BERT HUDD	Howard Lang
ROSE HUDD	Vivien Merchant
MR KIDD	Henry Woolf
MR SANDS	John Rees
MRS SANDS	Auriol Smith
RILEY	Thomas Baptiste

Directed by Harold Pinter

The Room was presented at The Royal Court Theatre on 8 March 1960 with the following cast:

BERT HUDD   Michael Brennan
ROSE HUDD   Vivien Merchant
MR KIDD   John Cater
MR SANDS   Michael Caine
MRS SANDS   Anne Bishop
RILEY   Thomas Baptiste

Directed by Anthony Page

Scene: a room in a large house. A door down right.
A gas-fire down left. A gas-stove and sink, up left.
A window up centre. A table and chairs, centre.
A rocking-chair, left centre. The foot of a double-bed
protrudes from alcove, up right.

BERT *is at the table, wearing a cap, a magazine*
propped in front of him. ROSE *is at the stove.*

ROSE
Here you are. This'll keep the cold out.

She places bacon and eggs on a plate, turns off the gas
and takes the plate to the table.

It's very cold out, I can tell you. It's murder.

She returns to the stove and pours water from the
kettle into the teapot, turns off the gas and brings the
teapot to the table, pours salt and sauce on the plate
and cuts two slices of bread. BERT *begins to eat.*

That's right. You eat that. You'll need it. You can feel
it in here. Still, the room keeps warm. It's better than
the basement, anyway.

She butters the bread.

I don't know how they live down there. It's asking for trouble. Go on. Eat it up. It'll do you good.

She goes to the sink, wipes a cup and saucer and brings them to the table.

If you want to go out you might as well have something inside you. Because you'll feel it when you get out.

She pours milk into the cup.

Just now I looked out of the window. It was enough for me. There wasn't a soul about. Can you hear the wind?

She sits in the rocking-chair.

I've never seen who it is. Who is it? Who lives down there? I'll have to ask, I mean, you might as well know, Bert. But whoever it is, it can't be too cosy. Did you ever see the walls? They were running. This is all right for me. Go on, Bert. Have a bit more bread.

She goes to the table and cuts a slice of bread.

I'll have some cocoa on when you come back.

She goes to the window and settles the curtain.

No, this room's all right for me. I mean, you know
where you are. When it's cold, for instance.

She goes to the table.

What about the rasher? Was it all right? It was a good
one, I know, but not as good as the last lot I got in.
It's the weather.

She goes to the rocking-chair, and sits.

Anyway, I haven't been out. I haven't been so well.
I didn't feel up to it. Still, I'm much better today.
I don't know about you though. I don't know whether
you ought to go out. I mean, you shouldn't, straight
after you've been laid up. Still. Don't worry, Bert. You
go. You won't be long.

She rocks.

It's good you were up here, I can tell you. It's good
you weren't down there, in the basement. That's no
joke. Oh, I've left the tea. I've left the tea standing.

She goes to the table and pours tea into the cup.

No, it's not bad. Nice weak tea. Lovely weak tea.
Here you are. Drink it down. I'll wait for mine.
Anyway, I'll have it a bit stronger.

She goes to the rocking-chair and sits.

If they ever ask you, Bert, I'm quite happy where I am. We're quiet, we're all right. You're happy up here. It's not far up either, when you come in from outside. And we're not bothered. And nobody bothers us.

Pause.

I don't know why you have to go out. Couldn't you run it down tomorrow? I could put the fire on later. You could sit by the fire. That's what you like, Bert, of an evening. It'll be dark in a minute as well, soon.

She rocks.

It gets dark now.

She rises and pours out tea at the table.

I made plenty. Go on.

She sits at table.

You looked out today? It's got ice on the roads. Oh, I know you can drive. I'm not saying you can't drive. I mentioned to Mr Kidd this morning that you'd be doing a run today. I told him you hadn't been too grand, but I said, still, he's a marvellous driver. I wouldn't mind what time, where, nothing, Bert. You know how to drive. I told him.

She wraps her cardigan about her.

But it's cold. It's really cold today, chilly. I'll have you some nice cocoa on for when you get back.

She rises, goes to the window, and looks out.

It's quiet. Be coming on for dark. There's no one about.

She stands, looking.

Wait a minute.

Pause.

I wonder who that is.

Pause.

No. I thought I saw someone.

Pause.

No.

She drops the curtain.

You know what though? It looks a bit better. It's not so windy. You'd better put on your thick jersey.

She goes to the rocking-chair, sits and rocks.

This is a good room. You've got a chance in a place like this. I look after you, don't I, Bert? Like when they offered us the basement here I said no straight off. I knew that'd be no good. The ceiling right on top of you. No, you've got a window here, you can move yourself, you can come home at night, if you have to go out, you can do your job, you can come home, you're all right. And I'm here. You stand a chance.

Pause.

I wonder who has got it now. I've never seen them, or heard of them. But I think someone's down there. Whoever's got it can keep it. That looked a good rasher, Bert. I'll have a cup of tea later. I like mine a bit stronger. You like yours weak.

A knock at the door. She stands.

Who is it?

Pause.

Hallo!

Knock repeated.

Come in then.

Knock repeated.

Who is it?

Pause. The door opens and MR KIDD *comes in.*

MR KIDD

I knocked.

ROSE

I heard you.

MR KIDD

Eh?

ROSE

We heard you.

MR KIDD

Hallo, Mr Hudd, how are you, all right? I've been looking at the pipes.

ROSE

Are they all right?

MR KIDD

Eh?

ROSE

Sit down, Mr Kidd.

MR KIDD

No, that's all right. I just popped in, like, to see how things were going. Well, it's cosy in here, isn't it?

ROSE

Oh, thank you, Mr Kidd.

MR KIDD

You going out today, Mr Hudd? I went out. I came
straight in again. Only to the corner, of course.

ROSE

Not many people about today, Mr Kidd.

MR KIDD

So I thought to myself, I'd better have a look at those
pipes. In the circumstances. I only went to the corner,
for a few necessary items. It's likely to snow. Very
likely, in my opinion.

ROSE

Why don't you sit down, Mr Kidd?

MR KIDD

No, no, that's all right.

ROSE

Well, it's a shame you have to go out in this weather,
Mr Kidd. Don't you have a help?

MR KIDD

Eh?

ROSE

I thought you had a woman to help.

MR KIDD

I haven't got any woman.

ROSE

I thought you had one when we first came.

MR KIDD

No women here.

ROSE

Maybe I was thinking of somewhere else.

MR KIDD

Plenty of women round the corner. Not here though.
Oh no. Eh, have I seen that before?

ROSE

What?

MR KIDD

That chair.

ROSE

I don't know. Have you?

MR KIDD

I seem to have some remembrance.

ROSE

It's just an old rocking-chair.

MR KIDD

Was it here when you came?

ROSE

No, I brought it myself.

MR KIDD

I could swear blind I've seen that before.

ROSE

Perhaps you have.

MR KIDD

What?

ROSE

I say, perhaps you have.

MR KIDD

Yes, maybe I have.

ROSE

Take a seat, Mr Kidd.

MR KIDD

I wouldn't take an oath on it though.

BERT *yawns and stretches, and continues looking at his magazine.*

No, I won't sit down, with Mr Hudd just having a bit
of a rest after his tea. I've got to go and get mine
going in a minute. You're going out then, Mr Hudd?
I was just looking at your van. She's a very nice little
van, that. I notice you wrap her up well for the cold.
I don't blame you. Yes, I was hearing you go off,
when was it, the other morning, yes. Very smooth.
I can tell a good gear-change.

ROSE

I thought your bedroom was at the back, Mr Kidd.

MR KIDD

My bedroom?

ROSE

Wasn't it at the back? Not that I ever knew.

MR KIDD

I wasn't in my bedroom.

ROSE

Oh, well.

MR KIDD

I was up and about.

ROSE

I don't get up early in this weather. I can take my
time. I take my time.

Pause.

MR KIDD

This was my bedroom.

ROSE

This? When?

MR KIDD

When I lived here.

ROSE

I didn't know that.

MR KIDD

I will sit down for a few ticks.

He sits in the armchair.

ROSE

Well, I never knew that.

MR KIDD

Was this chair here when you came?

ROSE

Yes.

MR KIDD

I can't recollect this one.

Pause.

ROSE

When was that then?

MR KIDD

Eh?

ROSE

When was this your bedroom?

MR KIDD

A good while back.

Pause.

ROSE

I was telling Bert I was telling you how he could drive.

MR KIDD

Mr Hudd? Oh, Mr Hudd can drive all right. I've seen him bowl down the road all right. Oh yes.

ROSE

Well, Mr Kidd, I must say this is a very nice room. It's a very comfortable room.

MR KIDD

Best room in the house.

ROSE

It must get a bit damp downstairs.

MR KIDD

Not as bad as upstairs.

ROSE

What about downstairs?

MR KIDD

Eh?

ROSE

What about downstairs?

MR KIDD

What about it?

ROSE

Must get a bit damp.

MR KIDD

A bit. Not as bad as upstairs though.

ROSE

Anyone live up there?

MR KIDD

Up there? There was. Gone now.

ROSE

How many floors you got in this house?

MR KIDD

Floors. (*He laughs.*) Ah, we had a good few of them in the old days.

ROSE

How many have you got now?

MR KIDD

Well, to tell you the truth, I don't count them now.

ROSE

Oh.

MR KIDD

No, not now.

ROSE

It must be a bit of a job.

MR KIDD

Oh, I used to count them, once. Never got tired of it. I used to keep a tack on everything in this house. I had a lot to keep my eye on, then. I was able for it too. That was when my sister was alive. But I lost track a bit, after she died. She's been dead some time now, my sister. It was a good house then. She was a capable woman. Yes. Fine size of a woman too. I think she took after my mum. Yes, I think she took after my old mum, from what I can recollect. I think my mum was a Jewess. Yes, I wouldn't be surprised to learn that she was a Jewess. She didn't have many babies.

ROSE

What about your sister, Mr Kidd?

MR KIDD

What about her?

ROSE

Did she have any babies?

MR KIDD

Yes, she had a resemblance to my old mum, I think.
Taller, of course.

ROSE

When did she die then, your sister?

MR KIDD

Yes, that's right, it was after she died that I must have
stopped counting. She used to keep things in very
good trim. And I gave her a helping hand. She was
very grateful, right until her last. She always used
to tell me how much she appreciated all the – little
things – that I used to do for her. Then she copped it.
I was her senior. Yes, I was her senior. She had a
lovely boudoir. A beautiful boudoir.

ROSE

What did she die of?

Pause.

MR KIDD

I've made ends meet.

Pause.

ROSE

You full at the moment, Mr Kidd?

MR KIDD

Packed out.

ROSE

All sorts, I suppose?

MR KIDD

Oh yes, I make ends meet.

ROSE

We do, too, don't we, Bert?

Pause.

Where's your bedroom now then, Mr Kidd?

MR KIDD

Me? I can take my pick. (*rising*) You'll be going out soon then, Mr Hudd? Well, be careful how you go. Those roads'll be no joke. Still, you know how to manipulate your van all right, don't you? Where you going? Far? Be long?

ROSE

He won't be long.

MR KIDD

No, of course not. Shouldn't take him long.

ROSE

No.

MR KIDD

Well then, I'll pop off. Have a good run, Mr Hudd.
Mind how you go. It'll be dark soon too. But not for
a good while yet. Arivederci.

He exits.

ROSE

I don't believe he had a sister, ever.

She takes the plate and cup to the sink. BERT *pushes
his chair back and rises.*

All right. Wait a minute. Where's your jersey?

She brings the jersey from the bed.

Here you are. Get into it.

She helps him into his jersey.

Right. Where's your muffler?

She brings a muffler from the bed.

Here you are. Wrap it round. That's it. Don't go too
fast, Bert, will you? I'll have some cocoa on when you
get back. You won't be long. Wait a minute. Where's
your overcoat? You'd better put on your overcoat.

*He fixes his muffler, goes to the door and exits. She
stands, watching the door, then turns slowly to the
table, picks up the magazine, and puts it down. She
stands and listens, goes to the fire, bends, lights the
fire and warms her hands. She stands and looks about
the room. She looks at the window and listens, goes
quickly to the window, stops and straightens the
curtain. She comes to the centre of the room, and
looks towards the door. She goes to the bed, puts on a
shawl, goes to the sink, takes a bin from under the
sink, goes to the door and opens it.*

Oh!

MR *and* MRS SANDS *are disclosed on the landing.*

MRS SANDS
So sorry. We didn't mean to be standing here, like.
Didn't mean to give you a fright. We've just come up
the stairs.

ROSE
That's all right.

MRS SANDS

This is Mr Sands. I'm Mrs Sands.

ROSE

How do you do?

MR SANDS *grunts acknowledgement.*

MRS SANDS

We were just going up the stairs. But you can't see a thing in this place. Can you, Toddy?

MR SANDS

Not a thing.

ROSE

What were you looking for?

MRS SANDS

The man who runs the house.

MR SANDS

The landlord. We're trying to get hold of the landlord.

MRS SANDS

What's his name, Toddy?

ROSE

His name's Mr Kidd.

MRS SANDS

Kidd. Was that the name, Toddy?

MR SANDS

Kidd? No, that's not it.

ROSE

Mr Kidd. That's his name.

MR SANDS

Well, that's not the bloke we're looking for.

ROSE

Well, you must be looking for someone else.

Pause.

MR SANDS

I suppose we must be.

ROSE

You look cold.

MRS SANDS

It's murder out. Have you been out?

ROSE

No.

MRS SANDS

We've not long come in.

ROSE

Well, come inside, if you like, and have a warm.
(*bringing the chair from the table to the fire*) Sit down
here. You can get a good warm.

MRS SANDS

Thanks. (*She sits.*)

ROSE

Come over by the fire, Mr Sands.

MR SANDS

No, it's all right. I'll just stretch my legs.

MRS SANDS

Why? You haven't been sitting down.

MR SANDS

What about it?

MRS SANDS

Well, why don't you sit down?

MR SANDS

Why should I?

MRS SANDS

You must be cold.

MR SANDS

I'm not.

MRS SANDS

You must be. Bring over a chair and sit down.

MR SANDS

I'm all right standing up, thanks.

MRS SANDS

You don't look one thing or the other standing up.

MR SANDS

I'm quite all right, Clarissa.

ROSE

Clarissa? What a pretty name.

MRS SANDS

Yes, it is nice, isn't it? My father and mother gave it to me.

Pause.

You know, this is a room you can sit down and feel cosy in.

MR SANDS

(*looking at the room*) It's a fair size, all right.

MRS SANDS

Why don't you sit down, Mrs –

ROSE

Hudd. No thanks.

MR SANDS

What did you say?

ROSE

When?

MR SANDS

What did you say the name was?

ROSE

Hudd.

MR SANDS

That's it. You're the wife of the bloke you mentioned
then?

MRS SANDS

No, she isn't. That was Mr Kidd.

MR SANDS

Was it? I thought it was Hudd.

MRS SANDS

No, it was Kidd. Wasn't it, Mrs Hudd?

ROSE

That's right. The landlord.

MRS SANDS

No, not the landlord. The other man.

ROSE

Well, that's his name. He's the landlord.

MR SANDS

Who?

ROSE

Mr Kidd.

Pause.

MR SANDS

Is he?

MRS SANDS

Maybe there are two landlords.

Pause.

MR SANDS

That'll be the day.

MRS SANDS

What did you say?

MR SANDS

I said that'll be the day.

Pause.

ROSE

What's it like out?

MRS SANDS

It's very dark out.

MR SANDS

No darker than in.

MRS SANDS

He's right there.

MR SANDS

It's darker in than out, for my money.

MRS SANDS

There's not much light in this place, is there, Mrs Hudd?
Do you know, this is the first bit of light we've seen
since we came in?

MR SANDS

The first crack.

ROSE

I never go out at night. We stay in.

MRS SANDS

Now I come to think of it, I saw a star.

MR SANDS

You saw what?

MRS SANDS

Well, I think I did.

MR SANDS

You think you saw what?

MRS SANDS

A star.

MR SANDS

Where?

MRS SANDS

In the sky.

MR SANDS

When?

MRS SANDS

As we were coming along.

MR SANDS

Go home.

MRS SANDS

What do you mean?

MR SANDS

You didn't see a star.

MRS SANDS

Why not?

MR SANDS

Because I'm telling you. I'm telling you you didn't see a star.

ROSE

I hope it's not too dark out. I hope it's not too icy. My husband's in his van. He doesn't drive slow either. He never drives slow.

MR SANDS

(*guffawing*) Well, he's taking a big chance tonight then.

ROSE

What?

MR SANDS

No – I mean, it'd be a bit dodgy driving tonight.

ROSE

He's a very good driver.

Pause.

How long have you been here?

MRS SANDS

I don't know. How long have we been here, Toddy?

MR SANDS

About half an hour.

MRS SANDS

Longer than that, much longer.

MR SANDS

About thirty-five minutes.

ROSE

Well, I think you'll find Mr Kidd about somewhere.
He's not long gone to make his tea.

MR SANDS

He lives here, does he?

ROSE

Of course he lives here.

MR SANDS

And you say he's the landlord, is he?

ROSE

Of course he is.

MR SANDS

Well, say I wanted to get hold of him, where would
I find him?

ROSE

Well – I'm not sure.

MR SANDS

He lives here, does he?

ROSE

Yes, but I don't know –

MR SANDS

You don't know exactly where he hangs out?

ROSE

No, not exactly.

MR SANDS

But he does live here, doesn't he?

Pause.

MRS SANDS

This is a very big house, Toddy.

MR SANDS

Yes, I know it is. But Mrs Hudd seems to know Mr
Kidd very well.

ROSE

No, I wouldn't say that. As a matter of fact, I don't
know him at all. We're very quiet. We keep ourselves
to ourselves. I never interfere. I mean, why should I?
We've got our room. We don't bother anyone else.
That's the way it should be.

MRS SANDS

It's a nice house, isn't it? Roomy.

ROSE

I don't know about the house. We're all right, but
I wouldn't mind betting there's a lot wrong with this
house.

She sits in the rocking-chair.

I think there's a lot of damp.

MRS SANDS

Yes, I felt a bit of damp when we were in the basement
just now.

ROSE

You were in the basement?

MRS SANDS

Yes, we went down there when we came in.

ROSE

Why?

MRS SANDS

We were looking for the landlord.

ROSE

What was it like down there?

MR SANDS

Couldn't see a thing.

ROSE

Why not?

MR SANDS

There wasn't any light.

ROSE

But what was – you said it was damp?

MRS SANDS

I felt a bit, didn't you, Tod?

MR SANDS

Why? Haven't you ever been down there, Mrs Hudd?

ROSE

Oh yes, once, a long time ago.

MR SANDS

Well, you know what it's like then, don't you?

ROSE

It was a long time ago.

MR SANDS

You haven't been here all that long, have you?

ROSE

I was just wondering whether anyone was living down
there now.

MRS SANDS

Yes. A man.

ROSE

A man?

MRS SANDS

Yes.

ROSE

One man?

MR SANDS

Yes, there was a bloke down there, all right.

He perches on the table.

MRS SANDS

You're sitting down!

MR SANDS

(*jumping up*) Who is?

MRS SANDS

You were.

MR SANDS

Don't be silly. I perched.

MRS SANDS

I saw you sit down.

MR SANDS

You did not see me sit down because I did not sit
bloody well down. I perched!

MRS SANDS

Do you think I can't perceive when someone's sitting
down?

MR SANDS

Perceive! That's all you do. Perceive.

MRS SANDS

You could do with a bit more of that instead of all
that tripe you get up to.

MR SANDS

You don't mind some of that tripe!

MRS SANDS

You take after your uncle, that's who you take after!

MR SANDS

And who do you take after?

MRS SANDS

I didn't bring you into the world.

MR SANDS

You didn't what?

MRS SANDS

I said, I didn't bring you into the world.

MR SANDS

Well, who did then? That's what I want to know.
Who did? Who did bring me into the world?

She sits, muttering. He stands, muttering.

ROSE

You say you saw a man downstairs, in the basement?

MRS SANDS

Yes, Mrs Hudd, you see, the thing is, Mrs Hudd, we'd
heard they'd got a room to let here, so we thought
we'd come along and have a look. Because we're
looking for a place, you see, somewhere quiet, and we
knew this district was quiet, and we passed the house
a few months ago and we thought it looked very nice,
but we thought we'd call of an evening, to catch the
landlord, so we came along this evening. Well, when
we got here we walked in the front door and it was
very dark in the hall and there wasn't anyone about.
So we went down to the basement. Well, we got down
there only due to Toddy having such good eyesight
really. Between you and me, I didn't like the look of it
much, I mean the feel, we couldn't make much out, it
smelt damp to me. Anyway, we went through a kind
of partition, then there was another partition, and we
couldn't see where we were going, well, it seemed to
me it got darker the more we went, the further we
went in, I thought we must have come to the wrong
house. So I stopped. And Toddy stopped. And then
this voice said, this voice came – it said – well, it gave

me a bit of a fright, I don't know about Tod, but
someone asked if he could do anything for us. So Tod
said we were looking for the landlord and this man
said the landlord would be upstairs. Then Tod asked
was there a room vacant. And this man, this voice
really, I think he was behind the partition, said
yes there was a room vacant. He was very polite,
I thought, but we never saw him, I don't know why
they never put a light on. Anyway, we got out then
and we came up and we went to the top of the house.
I don't know whether it was the top. There was a
door locked on the stairs, so there might have been
another floor, but we didn't see anyone, and it was
dark, and we were just coming down again when you
opened your door.

ROSE

You said you were going up.

MRS SANDS

What?

ROSE

You said you were going up before.

MRS SANDS

No, we were coming down.

ROSE

You didn't say that before.

MRS SANDS

We'd been up.

MR SANDS

We'd been up. We were coming down.

Pause.

ROSE

This man, what was he like, was he old?

MRS SANDS

We didn't see him.

ROSE

Was he old?

Pause.

MR SANDS

Well, we'd better try to get hold of this landlord,
if he's about.

ROSE

You won't find any rooms vacant in this house.

MR SANDS

Why not?

ROSE

Mr Kidd told me. He told me.

MR SANDS

Mr Kidd?

ROSE

He told me he was full up.

MR SANDS

The man in the basement said there was one. One
room. Number seven he said.

Pause.

ROSE

That's this room.

MR SANDS

We'd better go and get hold of the landlord.

MRS SANDS

(*rising*) Well, thank you for the warm-up, Mrs Hudd.
I feel better now.

ROSE

This room is occupied.

MR SANDS

Come on.

MRS SANDS

Goodnight, Mrs Hudd. I hope your husband won't be
too long. Must be lonely for you, being all alone here.

MR SANDS

Come on.

They go out. ROSE *watches the door close, starts towards it, and stops. She takes the chair back to the table, picks up the magazine, looks at it, and puts it down. She goes to the rocking-chair, sits, rocks, stops, and sits still. There is a sharp knock at the door, which opens. Enter* MR KIDD.

MR KIDD

I came straight in.

ROSE

(*rising*) Mr Kidd! I was just going to find you. I've got to speak to you.

MR KIDD

Look here, Mrs Hudd, I've got to speak to you. I came up specially.

ROSE

There were two people in here just now. They said this room was going vacant. What were they talking about?

MR KIDD

As soon as I heard the van go I got ready to come and see you. I'm knocked out.

ROSE

What was it all about? Did you see those people?
How can this room be going? It's occupied. Did they
get hold of you, Mr Kidd?

MR KIDD

Get hold of me? Who?

ROSE

I told you. Two people. They were looking for the
landlord.

MR KIDD

I'm just telling you. I've been getting ready to come
and see you, as soon as I heard the van go.

ROSE

Well then, who were they?

MR KIDD

That's why I came up before. But he hadn't gone yet.
I've been waiting for him to go the whole weekend.

ROSE

Mr Kidd, what did they mean about this room?

MR KIDD

What room?

ROSE

Is this room vacant?

MR KIDD

Vacant?

ROSE

They were looking for the landlord.

MR KIDD

Who were?

ROSE

Listen, Mr Kidd, you are the landlord, aren't you?
There isn't any other landlord?

MR KIDD

What? What's that got to do with it? I don't know
what you're talking about. I've got to tell you, that's
all. I've got to tell you. I've had a terrible weekend.
You'll have to see him. I can't take it any more.
You've got to see him.

Pause.

ROSE

Who?

MR KIDD

The man. He's been waiting to see you. He wants to
see you. I can't get rid of him. I'm not a young man,
Mrs Hudd, that's apparent. It's apparent. You've got
to see him.

ROSE

See who?

MR KIDD

The man. He's downstairs now. He's been there the
whole weekend. He said that when Mr Hudd went
out I was to tell him. That's why I came up before.
But he hadn't gone yet. So I told him. I said he hasn't
gone yet. I said, well when he goes, I said, you can go
up, go up, have done with it. No, he says, you must
ask her if she'll see me. So I came up again, to ask you
if you'll see him.

ROSE

Who is he?

MR KIDD

How do I know who he is? All I know is he won't say
a word, he won't indulge in any conversation, just –
has he gone? That and nothing else. He wouldn't even
play a game of chess. All right, I said, the other night,
while we're waiting I'll play you a game of chess. You
play chess, don't you? I tell you, Mrs Hudd, I don't
know if he even heard what I was saying. He just lies
there. It's not good for me. He just lies there, that's
all, waiting.

ROSE

He lies there, in the basement?

MR KIDD

Shall I tell him it's all right, Mrs Hudd?

ROSE

But it's damp down there.

MR KIDD

Shall I tell him it's all right?

ROSE

That what's all right?

MR KIDD

That you'll see him.

ROSE

See him? I beg your pardon, Mr Kidd. I don't know him. Why should I see him?

MR KIDD

You won't see him?

ROSE

Do you expect me to see someone I don't know? With my husband not here too?

MR KIDD

But he knows you, Mrs Hudd, he knows you.

ROSE

How could he, Mr Kidd, when I don't know him?

MR KIDD

You must know him.

ROSE

But I don't know anybody. We're quiet here. We've just moved into this district.

MR KIDD

But he doesn't come from this district. Perhaps you knew him in another district.

ROSE

Mr Kidd, do you think I go around knowing men in one district after another? What do you think I am?

MR KIDD

I don't know what I think.

He sits.

I think I'm going off my squiff.

ROSE

You need rest. An old man like you. What you need is rest.

MR KIDD

He hasn't given me any rest. Just lying there. In the black dark. Hour after hour. Why don't you leave me be, both of you? Mrs Hudd, have a bit of pity. Please see him. Why don't you see him?

ROSE

I don't know him.

MR KIDD

You can never tell. You might know him.

ROSE

I don't know him.

MR KIDD

(*rising*) I don't know what'll happen if you don't see him.

ROSE

I've told you I don't know this man!

MR KIDD

I know what he'll do. I know what he'll do. If you don't see him now, there'll be nothing else for it, he'll come up on his own bat, when your husband's here, that's what he'll do. He'll come up when Mr Hudd's here, when your husband's here.

ROSE

He'd never do that.

MR KIDD

He would do that. That's exactly what he'll do. You don't think he's going to go away without seeing you, after he's come all this way, do you? You don't think that, do you?

ROSE

All this way?

MR KIDD

You don't think he's going to do that, do you?

Pause.

ROSE

He wouldn't do that.

MR KIDD

Oh yes. I know it.

Pause.

ROSE

What's the time?

MR KIDD

I don't know.

Pause.

ROSE

Fetch him. Quick. Quick!

MR KIDD *goes out.* ROSE *sits in the rocking-chair.*

After a few moments the door opens. Enter a blind
NEGRO. *He closes the door behind him, walks further,*
and feels with a stick till he reaches the armchair. He
stops.

RILEY

Mrs Hudd?

ROSE

You just touched a chair. Why don't you sit in it?

He sits.

RILEY

Thank you.

ROSE

Don't thank me for anything. I don't want you up here. I don't know who you are. And the sooner you get out the better.

Pause.

(*rising*) Well, come on. Enough's enough. You can take a liberty too far, you know. What do you want? You force your way up here. You disturb my evening. You come in and sit down here. What do you want?

He looks about the room.

What are you looking at? You're blind, aren't you? So what are you looking at? What do you think you've got here, a little girl? I can keep up with you. I'm one ahead of people like you. Tell me what you want and get out.

RILEY

My name is Riley.

ROSE

I don't care if it's – What? That's not your name.
That's not your name. You've got a grown-up woman
in this room, do you hear? Or are you deaf too?
You're not deaf too, are you? You're all deaf and
dumb and blind, the lot of you. A bunch of cripples.

Pause.

RILEY

This is a large room.

ROSE

Never mind about the room. What do you know
about this room? You know nothing about it. And
you won't be staying in it long either. My luck. I get
these creeps come in, smelling up my room. What do
you want?

RILEY

I want to see you.

ROSE

Well you can't see me, can you? You're a blind man.
An old, poor blind man. Aren't you? Can't see a
dickeybird.

Pause.

They say I know you. That's an insult, for a start.
Because I can tell you, I wouldn't know you to spit
on, not from a mile off.

Pause.

Oh, these customers. They come in here and stink the
place out. After a handout. I know all about it. And
as for you saying you know me, what liberty is that?
Telling my landlord too. Upsetting my landlord. What
do you think you're up to? We're settled down here,
cosy, quiet, and our landlord thinks the world of us,
we're his favourite tenants, and you come in and
drive him up the wall, and drag my name into it!
What did you mean by dragging my name into it,
and my husband's name? How did you know what
our name was?

Pause.

You've led him a dance, have you, this weekend?
You've got him going, have you? A poor, weak old
man, who lets a respectable house. Finished. Done for.
You push your way in and shove him about. And you
drag my name into it.

Pause.

Come on, then. You say you wanted to see me. Well,
I'm here. Spit it out or out you go. What do you
want?

RILEY

I have a message for you.

ROSE

You've got what? How could you have a message for
me, Mr Riley, when I don't know you and nobody
knows I'm here and I don't know anybody anyway.
You think I'm an easy touch, don't you? Well, why
don't you give it up as a bad job? Get off out of it.
I've had enough of this. You're not only a nut, you're
a blind nut and you can get out the way you came.

Pause.

What message? Who have you got a message from?
Who?

RILEY

Your father wants you to come home.

Pause.

ROSE

Home?

RILEY

Yes.

ROSE

Home? Go now. Come on. It's late. It's late.

RILEY

To come home.

ROSE

Stop it. I can't take it. What do you want? What do
you want?

RILEY

Come home, Sal.

Pause.

ROSE

What did you call me?

RILEY

Come home, Sal.

ROSE

Don't call me that.

RILEY

Come, now.

ROSE

Don't call me that.

RILEY

So now you're here.

ROSE

Not Sal.

RILEY

Now I touch you.

ROSE

Don't touch me.

RILEY

Sal.

ROSE

I can't.

RILEY

I want you to come home.

ROSE

No.

RILEY

With me.

ROSE

I can't.

RILEY

I waited to see you.

ROSE

Yes.

RILEY

Now I see you.

ROSE

Yes.

RILEY

Sal.

ROSE

Not that.

RILEY

So, now.

Pause.

So, now.

ROSE

I've been here.

RILEY

Yes.

ROSE

Long.

RILEY

Yes.

ROSE

The day is a hump. I never go out.

RILEY

No.

ROSE

I've been here.

RILEY

Come home now, Sal.

She touches his eyes, the back of his head and his temples with her hands. Enter BERT.

He stops at the door, then goes to the window and draws the curtains. It is dark. He comes to the centre of the room and regards the woman.

BERT

I got back all right.

ROSE

(*going towards him*) Yes.

BERT

I got back all right.

Pause.

ROSE

Is it late?

BERT

I had a good bowl down there.

Pause.

I drove her down, hard. They got it dark out.

ROSE

Yes.

BERT

Then I drove her back, hard. They got it very icy out.

ROSE

Yes.

BERT

But I drove her.

Pause.

I sped her.

Pause.

I caned her along. She was good. Then I got back.
I could see the road all right. There was no cars. One
there was. He wouldn't move. I bumped him. I got my
road. I had all my way. There again and back. They
shoved out of it. I kept on the straight. There was no
mixing it. Not with her. She was good. She went with
me. She don't mix it with me. I use my hand. Like
that. I get hold of her. I go where I go. She took me
there. She brought me back.

Pause.

I got back all right.

*He takes the chair from the table and sits to the left of
the Negro's chair, close to it. He regards the* NEGRO
*for some moments. Then with his foot he lifts the
armchair up. The* NEGRO *falls on to the floor.*

RILEY

Mr Hudd, your wife –

BERT

Lice!

BERT *kicks the Negro's head against the gas-stove
several times. The* NEGRO *lies still.* BERT *walks away.*

Silence.